ALICIA ALONSO
AT HOME AND ABROAD

ALICIA ALONSO
AT HOME AND ABROAD
BY
TANA DE GAMEZ

With an Appreciation of the Artist
by
ARNOLD L. HASKELL

THE CITADEL PRESS, NEW YORK

First edition
Copyright © 1971 by Tana de Gámez
All rights reserved

Published by Citadel Press, Inc.
A subsidiary of Lyle Stuart, Inc.
222 Park Avenue South, New York, N.Y. 10003
In Canada: George J. McLeod Limited
73 Bathurst St., Toronto 2B, Ontario

Manufactured in the United States of America

Designed by Robert Fabian

Library of Congress catalog card number: 79-132703
ISBN 0-8065-0218-5

The lines of *Ballad of the Black Sorrow* by
Federico García Lorca are quoted in this
book by kind permission of
New Directions Publishing Corporation, New York.

Photo Credits

Archives of American Ballet Theatre, New York
Archives of Cuba's National Ballet
Archives of ICAIC, the Cuban Film Institute
Collection of the Martínez del Hoyo family, Havana
Collection of Osvaldo and Roberto Salas, Havana
The Tana de Gámez Collection, Boston University

Files of:

Dance magazine, New York
Le Monde, L'Express, Paris
Daily Telegraph, Daily Express, London
Tele-Express, Barcelona
Sociedad de Conciertos Daniel, Mexico
The Globe and Mail, Toronto
El Mundo, Prensa Latina, Havana
ABC Press, Amsterdam
Berlingske Tidende, Copenhagen

And, a distinguished roster of Cuban, Mexican, American and European photographers, too numerous to mention.

Acknowledgments

For the help and encouragement I received while planning this book, I want to express my profound gratitude to Lucia Chase and Florence Pettan of American Ballet Theatre; to dance historian Marian Eames, a friend of many years; to editors Lydia Joel and William Como of *Dance* magazine; to Genevieve Oswald, curator, and the staff of the Dance Collection, New York Public Library; to publishing consultant Frank O. Antonsanti; to Rina Romano, S. Hurok's representative in Mexico; to Arnold Haskell, my friend and collaborator whose enthusiasm set this project in motion from the moment I first told him about it; to the editors of Citadel Press and to Robert Fabian, the sensitive artist who designed this book; and above all to publisher Lyle Stuart, whose faith and vision made possible this long-time dream, and to John H. Hanlon, who spent countless hours dreaming it with me.

To Anne and Maxwell Geismar
for years of love and human concern.

Table of Contents

"Grace in all her steps, heaven in her eye,
In every gesture dignity and love."

John Milton: *Paradise Lost*

Presentation

For some time now, following a relaxation of cold war tensions, American audiences again have been permitted to extend their usual warm welcome to Soviet artists and musicians. Permitted is the operative word in this case. Indeed, it was the lowering of State Department restrictions that enabled impresario Sol Hurok to enrich our seasons once again with the Bolshoi and Kirov ballets, the Moiseyev and Don Cossaks' companies, the Moscow symphony and even the Russian circus. American official nod is also granted to the talent of other socialist nations. We are visited by folk and theatre companies from Rumania, Hungary, Yugoslavia; the films of Poland, Czechoslovakia and lately Hungary and Bulgaria find their way to our film houses with the same ease as those of France, Italy or Great Britain. Further to our rapprochement with the socialist world, at the time of this writing United States officials are resuming cool but far from hopeless negotiations with Communist China to initiate cultural relations.

In the middle of this accommodation to present day realities, the subject of this book continues to be the world's only great ballerina who is officially denied the right to perform for American audiences. Maya Plisetskaya of the Bolshoi is as free to dance in America and return to her homeland as is her British counterpart, Margot Fonteyn of the Royal Ballet, but Alicia Alonso of Cuba's National Ballet is not even allowed to set foot on our shores unless she defects from her country and renounces her national loyalties. Since ten years of private and official approaches have failed to produce that development, it is clear that we are unlikely to see Alonso dance in the United States in the forseeable future. We can do so in Paris, Montreal, Moscow, Barcelona, Brussels, Amsterdam, Tokyo or . . . Cuba, nowadays for U.S. citizens another planet which, thanks to State Department dispensation to journalists, the writer has been able to visit three times in the past six years.

Obviously, the blockade is on *us* this time; on the American public, on a generation of some of the best dancers and choreographers of our time, on the second largest and most knowledgeable dance audience in the world. Perhaps there is more grief than wrath in that official injustice.

Until Cuba took her back from us, Alonso was as ours as any American-born ballerina. It was in the United States that she developed as an artist, where she first found recognition and eventually stardom. She arrived in New York in the mid-thirties, Alicia Martínez del Hoyo, a teenaged ballerina one degree above a brilliant student, a middle-class runaway seeking liberation and professional status away from the limitations of a conventional Latin milieu. As fellow-rebel she had a young

Cuban aristocrat, Fernando Alonso. They had met and fallen in love in Havana, their hometown, while studying ballet under genteel, parent-supervised classes sponsored by an exclusive friends-of-music society. The young exiles married in New York, where their only child, a daughter, was born.

Alicia's professional debut was made in Broadway musicals (on the same chorus line with another unsuspected colossus-to-be of American ballet, Nora Kaye). Eventually the Alonsos joined Lincoln Kirstein's Ballet Caravan, genesis of today's New York City Ballet, directed by George Balanchine. In 1941 Alicia began her association with Lucia Chase's Ballet Theatre company; it lasted until her last performance in the United States, in the spring of 1960. It was in 1943, with Ballet Theatre, that she got her first chance to dance *Giselle,* the most coveted role in classical ballet, sharing it thereafter with the company's illustrious guest star, Markova. In and out of Ballet Theatre's precarious but durable existence—glorious to this day—there were several seasons with other companies, notably the Ballet Russe de Monte Carlo, where Alonso began her partnership with Igor Youskevitch, a team that was to generate a glamor and excitement only now being approached by that of Erik Bruhn and Carla Fracci.

By the mid-fifties Alonso was the Western world's indisputable *assoluta,* counterpart of Ulanova, her senior, in the East. She was the first Western ballerina to be invited to dance *Giselle* and *Swan Lake* in the Soviet Union.

As prima ballerina of our top companies during a golden era of ballet, Alonso exerted a tremendous influence on the American dance world. The most promising ballerinas of the time reflected the impact of her style. Vestiges of it can be seen in some of our classical stars today. A case in point is American Ballet Theatre's Lupe Serrano, who also resembles her somewhat.

Then, in 1960, while commanding one of the highest salaries in her field and top billing above all other ballet stars performing in America, Alicia Alonso decided to return permanently to her homeland, where for years she had been going back frequently to nurture the ranks and spirit of a struggling ballet bearing her name. It was the first year of the Cuban Revolution and few of her friends agreed with that decision. The consensus was that she could better serve her country by remaining the American *assoluta* and nonetheless a Cuban. "Too easy," was her answer. "I want to build a fine permanent company for my reborn land." (We remember our own misgivings at her parting.)

In two years the Alonsos had an internationally recognized Cuban company touring world capitals, Western and socialist, including appearances at the Bolshoi. In 1966, at the IV International Dance Festival in Paris, Cuba won two of the top prizes of the event, for the production and performance of *Giselle*. At Bulgaria's International Ballet Competitions, a flock of Cuban youngsters were scooping up medals every year, including the gold one awarded in 1968 to seventeen-year-old Jorge Esquivel, who elicited such predictions from critics as "the world's youngest promise of another Youskevitch." Esquivel was one of a group of waifs selected from Havana's orphanage in 1960 by the National Ballet Schools. By now, as the company's most promising male soloist, he is already partnering Alicia.

Whatever one's own feelings about the regime that fosters them, such achievements should warrant at least open appraisal. We are not asked to pass judgment on the system prevailing in Soviet Russia before we can enjoy her artists. But in the case of Cuba, even reading about those achievements—save in specialized publications—is often denied to us, since the majority of our daily press has chosen to reflect overwhelmingly the official U.S. policy of isolation towards Cuba (although we are told soon enough about hurricanes, shortages, and economic blunders). There are some notable exceptions, of course. *The New York Times*, for one, has published on occasion some excellent reports by Renata Adler, Juan de Onís and Richard Eder, dealing with various aspects of the Cuban reality, including its cultural gains. And yet, the same fine *New York Times* in 1967 published a cryptic review of Alicia Alonso's *Giselle* in Montreal, hailing the ballerina's "return" but failing to give a single indication as to where from or where to after the one-time performance, thus making an otherwise brilliant review sound like an account of a spatial creature's brief flight to earth from some awesome planet.

To our knowledge, only in specialized publications did one read, for instance, that in the 1967-68 Bolshoi season a Cuban-created and produced ballet joined the repertoire of Russia's *assoluta*, Maya Plisetskaya: *Carmen*, by Alberto Alonso, Cuba's National Ballet resident choreographer and Alicia's brother-in-law. And, admitted widely by Plisetskaya herself, this entirely new *Carmen* is her "most exciting and beloved role," as she puts it, adding Iberian vehemence to Slavic fire. It was tailored to her tremendous dynamics and brilliant personality. It has created a furor of delight and controversy in Europe. But whether we see Plisetskaya dance Alberto Alonso's *Carmen* in the United States depends on whether Mr. Hurok and the State Department will allow us a glimpse of Cuban talent by proxy of the Bolshoi. At the time of this writing the "privilege" is still under consideration. Traditionally the choreographer's country of origin and working base should be mentioned in the program, so . . . one word on a printed line seems to be holding up completion of the Bolshoi's repertoire for its next American season.

In the light of this unprecedented embargo—which surpasses even that of World War II on things German and Japanese—the prospects of Alicia Alonso dancing again for American audiences seem dismal indeed; because of her increasingly poor vision she is expected to retire prematurely from the performing stage. We must add that for the present her eye ailment does not at all affect her dancing. Although in her off-stage leisure she does welcome a chivalrous hand to lead the way, she continues to live a normal ballet-centered life, with all the glamor and public activities that go with the hard work and iron discipline.

In 1967 she got as close to us as sixty minutes by air from the New York that she loves and longs to see again. It was during Montreal's Expo, when she and her partner, Azari Plisetki (Maya's brother, by the way), were invited by Les Grands Ballets Canadiens to dance *Giselle*. Anton Dolin—her partner in her first, historic *Giselle*—was commissioned to stage the one-time production for the occasion. It was a memorable night. Walter Terry's report of it appeared in *Saturday Review* with all the pertinent facts: "Alicia Alonso, Cuban-born and American-trained ballerina of International fame . . . danced in Canada, and a striking segment of the audience in the huge, new Place des Arts in Montreal was made up of both illustrious and humble Alonso fans, of both those who knew well the brilliance of her art and those to whom she is a legend. She disappointed neither . . . Today Alonso remains one of the greatest Giselles you will ever see . . . The audience cheered to what in a less aristocratic house would be called the rafters . . . Alicia Alonso, Cuban ballerina, was almost back home in America again. But not quite."

Perhaps she'll be a bit closer to us now.

In this pictorial biography we review her life as a personality and as a ballerina, from her first dancing picture to her latest performances in Europe, with the Royal Danish Ballet in October of 1969. But she is a lot more than that. Alicia Alonso is a formidable spirit, a profoundly concerned humanist, a deeply engaged intellectual; a true artist of our changing age and one of the greatest of our time.

Tana de Gámez
New York
May 1970

This appreciation of Alicia Alonso is dedicated,
as she would wish, to her compatriots
whom she is serving and whom she taught
me to admire and to love.

A.L.H.

An Appreciation of the Artist and the Human Being

by Arnold L. Haskell

It is a truism to say that dancing is an ephemeral art. That is one of the reasons for the intense pleasure every moment of a great performance gives us. There is the feeling that here am I witnessing a moment of magic, something that will never happen again in exactly the same way. When one is fortunate enough to assist at the magic performance applause seems an intolerable intrusion, complete silence the only worthy tribute. Yet that shattering applause, unwelcome though it is, prolongs the pleasure. The artist takes her calls, postscripts to the performance in which she reveals still more of herself, her attitude to her art and her audience. Standing in front of the curtain, away from the world of illusion, the *wili* becomes a human being. Alas, at times too rapidly and too completely as she tugs at a tightly wired flower to offer her partner. The expedient lies in wait to break the spell. We think of the congestion at the cloakroom and the last train home.

In over half a century of watching ballet such moments of magic have been few. The adequate is not enough, it provides entertainment that lasts only as long as the action. The performance that is a real experience and that touches the emotions deeply lives on in the memory to be awakened by a few bars of music, a photograph, or a programme. It is the classical ballet that can alone set the scene for such magic, the rigid technical framework that must be tamed and mastered before the artist can emerge and reveal herself. It is through these familiar exercises —exercises one can only liken to the preparation for a mystical experience—that the ballerina disappears and becomes Giselle.

I write of *Giselle* because it has a dimension undreamed of by Gautier, Adam, or Saint-Léon. The ballerina can make it universal and ageless. My vivid memories are mainly involved with *Giselle;* Pavlova, who in all her roles showed some aspect of Giselle, in the innocent gaiety of *Christmas* as in the deep pathos of the *Dying Swan;* Markova as light as the brushstrokes of Corot; Spessivtseva as she handled the sword, a grand tragic figure; Chauviré and Ulanova, complete in portraying the rounded figure in which the *wili* is still the Giselle we first met in grape-harvest time. Each one of these was a mature artist, essential for such role.

If one is to write an appreciation of an artist, it is important to see her in the company of her peers. Alicia Alonso has her rightful place here among the very greatest.

I first saw Alonso when she danced *Giselle* with Ballet Theatre in London in the Summer of 1947. In looking over my notes of the period, I find that I was not greatly impressed. I wrote that, given a far better production, here was a dancer who could become a true Giselle. I was, with certain reservations, impressed by the fluency of her classical technique, but when writing of *Giselle* that is in a sense irrelevant.

It was many years later, when I saw her as Giselle *in her own production,* that I was carried away emotionally and realised the deeply serious thought that had gone into the work. It remains the only *complete Giselle* I have seen.

However great the interpreter, Giselle cannot exist in a vacuum. She is her mother's daughter, a girl in love, a girl subjected to the jealous passion of a boorish peasant, the unwitting rival of a princess. Of all these factors of her character the most important in the first act is her relationship to her aristocratic rival, Bathilde. In every production I have seen, until that of Cuba's National Ballet, Bathilde is a non-character. All one can remember is a velvet dress and a plumed hat worn by a tall and usually a pretty girl. Gautier himself realised the importance of the character and wrote a poem to Bathilde in which he reveals that in the end she becomes Albrecht's bride. There is no dramatic balance without a positive Bathilde, one who is disdainful, patronising and, in the end—when the peasant girl has ceased to amuse her and dares to become her rival—who cannot for a moment imagine that a mere peasant has the right to have any feelings at all. It is this contrast that turns all our sympathy to Giselle. Alicia Alonso both felt and understood this and produced a magnificent foil in Loipa Araujo, the first flesh and blood Bathilde I have seen.

It is this rare understanding of the ballet as a whole that makes Alonso's performance of *Giselle* unique. There is complete communication between every character in the drama. Another feature of this performance is the strength, precision and sense of immense power held in reserve in Alonso's classical technique. It is, of course, impossible to be a Giselle at all without a commanding technique, but such technical precision by itself can serve as a handicap in the role. It is all too often a tug of war between the ballerina and the simple and loving village maiden. The ballerina is a star, used to taking absolute command of the stage from her moment of entry and to dazzle the audience by the sheer difficulty of her steps. Giselle is an innocent. She loves and she suffers. In this role Alicia becomes Giselle from her very entrance and masters her own vivid temperament, making her quite exceptional virtuosity serve the character. And I know of no greater purely classical virtuoso in ballet at this time.

Alicia Alonso is not a one character ballerina. Take her Swanilda in *Coppelia,* for instance. This is a *soubrette* role in which in most cases the dramatic, highly technical dancer of vivid personality usually fails. It is often best performed by a very young dancer; its creator was a seventeen year old. It is, so to speak, a *blonde*, a coloratura role. I had considerable misgivings when I heard that Alicia was to be Swanilda. Here again from her very first entrance the character was established; young, mischievous and a flirt. It is in a sense a very flat character, indeed scarcely a character at all. Swanilda is usually as much a doll as the Coppélia she impersonates. Alicia gave it a piquant quality. She was a woman, bent on getting her own way, ruthless, even a trifle malicious in her dealings with the old magician, half comic, half sinister.

There are other entire changes of personality in Alonso. Anton Dolin's evocative *Pas de Quatre* is a very charming, nostalgic pastiche rather than a reproduction of one of ballet's historic moments. It is exceedingly difficult to bring off, if it is to be more than a *tableau vivant* based on a romantic lithograph. To dance it is comparatively simple; its usual atmosphere—and I have seen it with a score of casts—is to exaggerate, to give a broad performance, a burlesque that offends because it patronises the great artists of the past. The lithographs of the period are in no sense realistic, they are not outstanding works of art. In fact, they are sentimental and quaint, therein lies their appeal, which is considerable. Alonso is never sentimental, she is romantic, she transcends these lithographs to pay a very genuine tribute to Taglioni, her great sister of a former generation. And here again there is this understanding of the work as a whole in which her fellow artists, whatever cast she may select, are all on the same wave length. No archness, no pandering to applause, complete simplicity and serenity. The magic works in rehearsal, without the effective period dressing.

Another character emerges from this magical blend of mood, temperament and style: Alicia in *Carmen*, Alberto Alonso's controversial ballet. This is not a realistic work in the sense of Roland Petit's brilliant creation of the same name. It attempts no direct narrative, it deals with symbols in the same way that Robert Helpmann did in his *Hamlet* . The bull ring itself is the arena of life, brutal and passionate, a contest between life and death, love and hate, the positive and the negative. The subject matter is difficult in the extreme. The slightest error in interpretation makes it not only obscure but distasteful and even ridiculous. It deals with sex but it is not "sexy," it requires a tightrope balance. And I do not believe that the re-orchestrated score assists it in any way. It is a moot point from the start whether an opera should be transformed into a ballet, especially when the work of a master is distorted. Skilled as it is, Schedrin's orchestration seems to me to overemphasize the drama, making what should be left to the dancers to interpret so much more difficult.

Here again Alonso's extraordinary restraint, her mastery over her own vivid personality and essentially Latin temperament is triumphantly successful. A wriggling, hipwagging Carmen is easily transformed in a cabaret act. The Spanish dancer herself is alluring but never vulgar; she has an inherent dignity, tremendous strength that must not be dissipated in meaningless sex-kitten distortions. Carmen is a seductress in the grand manner, never a tart. She must show a subtle yet definite difference in her attitude towards the weak Don José and the all-conquering bullfighter. All of which is realised in Alicia Alonso's interpretation. After it is all over and the applause has died down, one can only marvel at the transformation of this highly classical dancer and the extraordinary technical difficulties she has overcome.

In these roles I have chosen for discussions, each one so dissimilar, there are certain common factors; the complete grasp of the ballet as a whole and the interdependence of the characters, which in itself makes Alonso unique in my experience, her absolute understanding of herself and the total mastery of a very vivid personality, a sign of humility, and the extraordinary feeling of great power held in reserve. This last quality can be seen in the classroom in the performance of a complex and in itself meaningless *enchainement*.

It is fascinating to follow Alicia into the classroom and onto the rehearsal stage. Her husband, Fernando Alonso, Director of Cuba's National Ballet, is a creative teacher for whom a class of fifteen dancers becomes private lessons. He is meticulous in his corrections, a scientist and an artist. These Alonsos are essentially a team. There are no half measures about Alicia in the classroom. She tries for quantity and quality and these performances dazzle by their sheer textbook perfection. She challenges, rivals and surpasses her own brilliant young ballerinas, "Cuba's jewels," Mirta Pla, Josefina Méndez, Loipa Araujo, Aurora Bosch. It is remarkable that not one of them is a pale imitation of the company's *assoluta*, It has not come about by chance. The Alonsos have studied each one as an individual. At rehearsal Alicia demonstrates each role, stressing this vital question of interdependence. In any change of cast she can and does vary her interpretation to fit in with the different environment.

I have only seen one work by Alicia as choreographer rather than producer, her ballet *Circus*, which she dismisses lightly as a children's entertainment. Is is a work of close observation and a very complete translation from one form of art into another, delicate, witty and with circus magic seen entirely through a child's eyes. It stands with Petit's *Les Forains* as the only success among the innumerable attempts to pay tribute to the circus, Petit showing the pathos of the threadbare itinerant entertainers, Alonso the bright lights and the spangles.

The Cuban National Ballet, youngest of all the national schools that have grown since the flowering of ballet, is the creation of the Alonso family. Alicia and Fernando gained experience in the United States where she became a prima ballerina, excelling in the classics and creating many important dramatic roles in the ballets of Agnes de Mille and dancing in works by Tudor, Balanchine and Fokine. Alberto Alonso, the choreographer, worked with de Basil in the great days of de Basil's *ballet russe* revival. It is by no chance that his nickname was "Cuba." The Alonsos have always been staunch patriots. The idea of a national Cuban ballet grew out of a society, "Pro-Arte Musical," of which Fernando's and Alberto's mother was the moving force, much in the same way as the British ballet was fostered by the Camargo society. Alicia would make frequent journeys from the United States back to Cuba, lending her artistry and fame and spending her own money on the young company. It was a tremendous act of faith, not only in her own powers but in the future of her small country. The company survived, the finest teachers were brought over to train the dancers and to produce, the public grew in knowledge with the young dancers, but it was a continual financial struggle.

The Revolution gave the ballet its great opportunity, ample funds for a school on a scale that is the equal of any in the world, a generous subsidy for productions and for the holding of an annual dance festival that drew dancers from all over the world, including great stars of the Bolshoi and the Kirov. The world in general knew little of what was going on. The first astonishing break-through came with the International Ballet Competitions held at Varna, Bulgaria. Many questioned the purpose of such contest. They immediately justified themselves by the Cuban experience. These unknown young Cuban dancers, year after year, came second only to the Russians in the number of medals won, a success that was followed up in the great Moscow competition of 1969. These Cubans had arrived in a big way. Only someone who has watched them at home during several months can realise the tremendous work involved. The buildings are there, the subsidies are there, and the public is large and enthusiastic; at times it rivals a baseball crowd in its fervent partisanship. Alicia is "the first woman" in Cuba, a very symbol of its courage and independence. But the speed of success has brought fresh problems. Classes have grown; the provinces have started schools and companies; and the ballerinas not only dance and rehearse and travel, but each also has a class of her own, passing on the Alonsos' knowledge.

There is also a new element, the Afro-Cuban, to be assimilated into what has been for generations a purely white preserve. There is a new choreography that must include the folklore and dancing of Cuba and that has made an exciting start with Alberto Alonso's *El Güije (The Evil Spirit)* with the fantastic creole dancer Sonia Calero, Alberto's wife, in the leading role. Poets, composers and designers must make the ballet their own and Cuba is exceptionally rich in painters and poets, and with a folklore that includes Catholicism and Voodoo, Europe and Africa.

So far I have not written of Alicia Alonso as a person, though a personality has surely begun to emerge. I have not yet mentioned her great handicap, badly impaired eyesight, which in the forties kept her in complete darkness for over a year. It is irrelevant when one sees her dance but it has played a major role in her development as an artist. To suffer and to overcome has given her sympathy, understanding, courage, and complete self-confidence. In the performances that I saw great tribute must be paid to her partner, Azari Plisetski, a splendid artist on whom she can completely rely. Yet I have seen her dance with a comparative novice when only her intimates could have known the added strain. Her sense of space and her use of the stage are an outstanding feature of her work, as is the detailed preparation that allows her for instance to grasp the sword in *Giselle* without fumbling. Watching rehearsals, armed with a pair of binoculars, no detail escapes her.

My first reunion with Alicia came about in Bulgaria in the perfect setting of the Black Sea resort of Druzjba, where the large international jury was lodged. On the whole one saw less of her than of the others; she left early for class, she came back late from rehearsals. I have known these Cubans to rehearse in the big open air theatre at 4 A.M. Where I did see her was at our innumerable meetings and discussions that, on occasions, lasted until daylight. Alicia is a formidable debater; fluent, passionate, a stickler for the rules, yet with a consistency and logic that are not always obvious to those with a different opinion. This is not made easier by the number of languages through which the argument passes, though Alicia is fluent in English. Any sense of injustice to any dancer not necessarily Cuban rouses her to great eloquence. Once the argument is over, whether it has been decided in her favour or not, the matter rests, no heat remains, it has never been personal. Her self-discipline is complete.

Our friendship, begun in Varna, ripened in Cuba, which I visited on two occasions for three months, lecturing to the dancers and the public and becoming an unofficial member of the company. There I saw the artist and the person in a country that she taught me to love and to which she has contributed so much. There is Alicia at home romping with her dogs, surprisingly as 'doggy' a person as one could see, tweeded and brogued, in the English countryside. There are the Alonsos with their chickens, a not so miniature poultry farm. And always with Alicia one or two of her ballerinas, as much her daughters as her own beautiful Laura, or with some pupils from the school, all completely at ease, a true family. In spite of the acute partisanship of the public, there are no jealousies.

There is another Alicia, speaking at some rally or meeting, taking on some task that will enrich the leisure, such as it is, of her people. When she enters the theatre all rise spontaneously to applaud, there is a queue of autograph hunters; to all of them she is *Alicia*, their beloved *compañera*, there are no *Madames*, there is intimacy and respect. I see her at a *corps de ballet* birthday party or at a wedding, chatting with proud mothers or playing with the children. She may be, indeed she must be tired, but she never shows it. She is too closely identified with the life of the people to know what boredom means.

One of my most vivid memories is of Alicia as an agricultural worker. The bus leaves from the studio at 5:30 in the morning before the great heat of the day. Everyone in Cuba participates in some phase of the vast agricultural programme, the more muscular in the backbreaking work of cutting the sugar cane. The artists have been allotted a huge parcel of land in which to fill plastic bags with earth for planting of coffee. Alicia in a large peasant straw hat squats on the ground among her dancers and with a speed and a rhythm that, alas, I was never to achieve for all my willingness, she fills the bags, demanding more and more barrow loads of earth wheeled in by the boys. The sun burns down fiercely. Finally exhausted, I lie down placidly under a tree, smothered from head to foot in the black earth, while Alicia and her dancers plod on, laughing, joking and singing until the task is complete.

This contact with the Revolution, the people, and the soil has greatly enriched Alicia Alonso as a person and consequently as an artist. She will occupy a large place not only in the annals of ballet but in the history of Cuba.

Today and Yesterday

First Spanish dancing lesson, age 9, when her father took her with him on a business trip to Jerez de la Frontera, **Spain.**

Bluebird variation at age 11 in Havana.

Far right: At age 5: dancing the *Charleston* with her brothers and sister, during a family stay in Carlisle, Pennsylvania.

Echoes of Jerez de la
Frontera: *Don Quixote
pas de deux,* during an
American Ballet Theatre
season at the Metro-
politan Opera House,
circa 1948.

Ten years later, *Swan Lake,* with
American Ballet Theatre.

Her first ballet costume, *Sleeping
Beauty,* in a version staged by
Nikolai Yavorsky, one of her first
teachers. Havana, age 10.

Left: Alonso in *Carmen,* an entirely new ballet by the resident choreographer of Cuba's National Ballet, Alberto Alonso—her brother-in-law. This work was first produced at the Bolshoi for Maya Plisetskaya. "The Russian and Cuban ballerinas, indisputably *assolutas* in their respective national theatres, are now at the peak of their careers . . . It makes news in ballet when two such luminaries elect to create the same role."—Olga Maynard, *After Dark* magazine, New York, April 1969.

Above: at her Miramar home in Havana, December 1969, with her dogs Onyx and Diana.

A la Degas, age 20, in Havana.

Tap-dancing in *Stars in Your Eyes,* a Broadway musical of the late thirties. From the left, front line: chorines Maria Karnilova, Nora Kaye, and Alicia Alonso.

In another Broadway musical, *Great Lady.* From the right: Alicia, Fernando Alonso, and Nora Kaye.

Rehearsing in a vocal chorus, circa 1938.

We reproduce the original caption: "Headquarters, U.S. Air Base Rhein-Main, Public Information Office, APO 57 Frankfurt, Germany. For immediate release. Graceful sprites visiting a member of the 11th Troop Carrier Squadron, as he dozes against the wheel of a C-82. The sprites came to life at the Rhein-Main performance of August 14 before a very receptive crowd. Left to right: Nora Kaye and Alicia Alonso, ballerinas of the American Ballet Theatre company."

Presiding at a banquet with Ho Chi Minh in Hanoi, 1964, when the Cuban National Ballet performed in North Vietnam.

A hazy autumn morning in Paris, 1966, during the IV International Dance Festival, where Cuba won two of the top prizes of the event, the *prix de la ville de Paris,* and the Anna Pavlova award of the Dance University of Paris, both for Alicia's production of *Giselle.* She is seen in the center, surrounded by ballerinas of other nations.

Above: At the closing ceremonies of the IV International Dance Festival, Paris, 1966: French dancer-choreographer Serge Lifar and Cuban ballerinas Aurora Bosch and Alicia Alonso.

Right: Alicia, delivering one of the prizes she won to Dr. Baudilio Castellanos, Cuban ambassador to France in 1966. Aurora Bosch in the background.

Far right: "Today, Alonso remains one of the greatest Giselles you will ever see." —Walter Terry, *Saturday Review*, July 15, 1967.

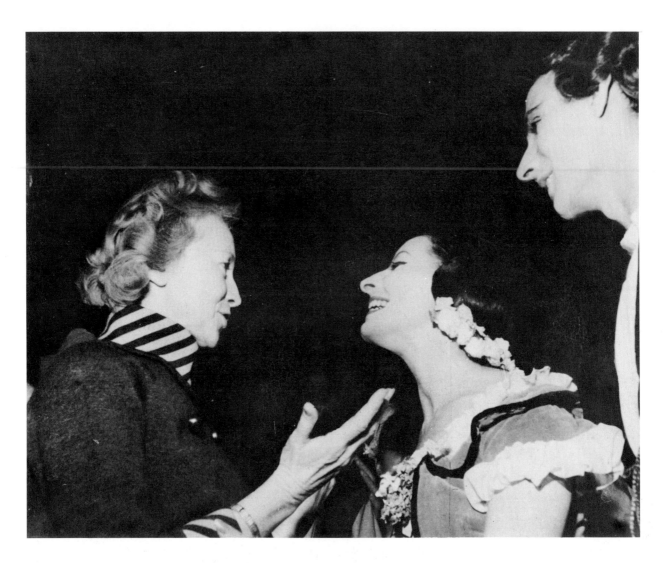

"Her dancing is something wonderfully classic and organic. I bow to her art," said Galina Ulanova, Russia's retired *assoluta,* seen here with Alicia and Plisetski during the IV International Dance Festival in Paris, 1966.

They were joined by French *assoluta*, Yvette Chauviré, and ballerina Liane Daydé.

A still from the 1965 production of *Giselle* by the
Cuban Film Institute, with Azari Plisetski as Albrecht.
A copy of this full-length version of the ballet
is now in the archives of the Dance Collection,
New York Public Library, at Lincoln Center for the
Performing Arts, donated by Alicia Alonso and
Cuba's National Ballet to the City of New York,
to be shown upon request.

It's cold backstage at the Bolshoi, and a tense but chivalrous husband provides what warmth he can. Awaiting one of her entrances.

40

Children of the tropics, Alicia and Fernando, enjoying the snow at Riga's open air theatre, 1957.

Back in the first lean days in New York. A sparsely furnished flat—presumably so they could practice. But there was a crib for Laura waiting in a closet; she was already expected.

Above: Laura, the Alonsos'
daughter, leading the Czardas
in *Coppélia* at Havana's García
Lorca theatre, 1969.

Upper left: the Alonsos at home
in Havana, circa 1952.

Left: Maya Plisetskaya and
Fernando Alonso look on as
Laura wishes her mother success
in *Carmen* at the Bolshoi, 1969.

A pause in the rehearsal, September 1961, with her beloved Champagne, now gone to dog heaven.

"How can such a delicate, ethereal creature have such a healthy, earthy laugh?" asked Premier Castro, backstage at Havana's García Lorca Theatre. Behind Alicia, her partner, Azari Plisetski, *premier danseur* of Cuba's National Ballet, after a performance of *Giselle*, 1967.

Circa 1955, with the dean of American dancers, Ted Shawn, and Danish *premier danseur* Erik Bruhn.

In 1957 Fernando's camera caught her trying to feed a reluctant swan in the gardens of Lisbon's royal palace. They were touring Europe then with the American Ballet Theatre.

46

Opposite: The same year, in Paris.

"Colin" carrying off his mischievous "Lise" in *La Fille Mal Gardée*, in a 1955 production in Havana.

"Alicia Alonso and Igor Youskevitch," a billing that had a magic and a box office draw unequaled in contemporary ballet. Rehearsing Antony Tudor's *Romeo and Juliet* at the Metropolitan Opera House, circa 1955.

"When I would complain about something she did not do according to our pre-arrangement, she would say: 'Please, Youssy, let me dance; please let me dance!'" the great Russian-American *danseur* reminisces about his brilliant days with the Cuban ballerina. They are seen here during one of their European tours of the fifties.

Above: A street scene in Ecuador, 1959.

Left: A culture-conscious pre-Batista government decorated her with the highest Cuban honor, the Order of Carlos Manuel de Céspedes. Shortly after, she received Uruguay's Order of Merit.

Far left, top: with American *danseur* Royes Fernández and British choreographer Mary Skeaping, who were brought to Havana in 1953 for a new production of *Swan Lake*.

Far left, below: Cecchetti Day in London, 1953, honoring the memory of the great Italian ballet master, Enrico Cecchetti, whose method revolutionized ballet early in this century. Alicia awarding prizes with Cyril Beaumont, the notable British dance writer and publisher.

51

Above: Composer Aram Kachaturian greeting the Cuban *assoluta* at a cocktail party in Moscow in 1969.

Upper right: Alicia and Fernando Alonso with members of Cuba's National Ballet as guests of Mao Tse Tung after a performance of *Giselle* in Peking, 1960.

Lower right: Arriving at Riga, 1957, during her first tour of the Soviet Union. She was the first Western ballerina invited by the Russians to dance *Swan Lake* and *Giselle*.

Above: As Swanilda in *Coppélia*, partnered
by South American *danseur* Hugo Guffanti,
during a gala performance for the delegates
to the Cultural Congress at Havana's Lorca
theatre. It was the first time that Arnold
Haskell was to see her in this role and he
admits to having had considerable misgivings.
"But here again, from her very first entrance
the character was established. . . . She was a
woman, bent on getting her own way, ruthless, even a trifle malicious in her dealings
with the old magician, half comic, half
sinister," he wrote the next morning.

Opposite: Alonso and Plisetski in *Don
Quixote pas de deux* performed in a natural
setting of the *settecento*, Havana's cathedral
plaza, boarded up for the occasion. The
symphony orchestra played on the steps
of the cathedral, the diplomatic corps and
other notables sat under the colonnades of
former palaces, which today are museums of
colonial art. The event was the opening of
Cuba's Cultural Congress, January 1968.

At Montreal's Place des Arts in 1967, Alonso and Plisetski taking their bows at the end of another historic *Giselle*. "The audience cheered her to what in a less aristocratic theatre would be called the rafters; the stage was covered with flowers. . . ." reported Walter Terry in *Saturday Review*.

Celebrating her birthday, December 21, in Shanghai, 1964.

With Chou En Lai, toasting after a performance in Peking, 1964.

Hanoi, 1964. Premier Pham Van Dong greets the Cuban *assoluta* back stage before a performance, during one of her tours of North Viet Nam.

In *The Urchin*, her own ballet about a crafty little character in pre-Revolutionary Havana who forages for tourists' tips and ends up cold and lonely, sleeping under the colonnades of the plaza of St. Christopher's cathedral. It was premiered right on the square's venerable cobblestones, with Alicia —thank old St. Chris—in soft shoe.

Yesterday: Her first public ballet
performance, in the waltz from
Sleeping Beauty, at the age of 10;
and on her eighth birthday,
in a postcard photo taken "for
my little grandmother."

Today: As the heroic
figure in Azari Plisetski's
ballet, *The Watchtower*,
performing for the troops
stationed in Guantanamo;
and as *Carmen*, a still from
her autobiographical film.

The Swans and Juliet

"When you dance, I wish you
A wave o' the sea, that you might ever do
Nothing but that."
Shakespeare: *The Winter's Tale*

Two stills from her biography, *Alicia*, a 1968 full-length production of the Cuban Film Institute containing excerpts from the most notable ballets in her repertoire. Here, Act III of *Swan Lake*, with Azari Plisetski as Prince Siegfried and Hugo Guffanti as Rothbart, the magician.

The "white swan" *pas de deux*,
ten years apart. With Azari Plisetski
in a sequence of the film *Alicia*,
taken in the gardens of Havana's
former Country Club—now a
school city called Cubanacán; and
with Igor Youskevitch, during the
1958 season of the American Ballet
Theatre in New York. Since the turn
of the century the *Lake* has been
one of the most durable virtuoso
roles of a prima ballerina, although
it was not very successful when it
was first produced in 1877 at the
Bolshoi. In fact, Tchaikowsky died
believing that his score for *Swan
Lake* had been a failure.

At the height of her stardom with the American Ballet Theatre, in the roles of Odette, the swan, and Odile, the impersonator. Like many romantic ballets in the classic repertoire, *Swan Lake* is based on a fairy tale. Siegfried, a young carefree prince, goes hunting for wild swans in an enchanted forest. There he meets a bewitching creature, Odette, Queen of the Swans, who has been condemned by an evil magician, Rothbart, to live in the shape of the languid birds who inhabit the lake. Only when she finds true love will the spell be broken. Just when that happy event seems near in the lovers' embrace, the magician appears and takes away the girl-swan. There is a ball at the castle that night. Pining for his newly found love, Prince Siegfried suddenly believes he has found her among the guests. Beside himself with joy, he dances with her and swears eternal love to her, only to discover that she is not Odette, but the magician's daughter, Odile, impersonating the sad, absent Swan Queen. Grieving his near-mortal mistake, the prince rushes to the lake, where he finds Odette about to kill herself. Together, the lovers defy the magician and succeed in breaking the spell. In some versions Siegfried and Rothbart engage in combat; in all of them love is triumphant in the end, and Odette and her prince live happily ever after in the kingdom beneath the lake.

Above: Behind the curtain at the
Metropolitan with Igor Youskevitch,
getting ready for the Black Swan
pas de deux with the American
Ballet Theatre in the mid-fifties.

Right: South African-born *danseur*
Michael Maule partnered her in the
classic repertoire during the 1949-50
season with Ballet Alicia Alonso. They
are seen here in *Swan Lake*, act II.

Left: With Azari Plisetski and the
cygnets, in the Cuban National Ballet
production of the *Lake*, Havana 1969.

Far left: Odile, a portrait taken
in Havana, circa 1950.

Portrait through prisms:
Odile's deception, a
montage from the film
Alicia, where she dances
several excerpts from
Swan Lake.

In Black Swan regalia at
the Salas studio in Havana,
December 1969.

The ball scene in *Swan Lake* at the Bolshoi, 1965, partnered by Sviatoslav Kuznetsov, in a full-length production of the ballet.

The famous profile in three swan moods

Left: A rare *Dying Swan*, a role she seldom dances. "I can't fully identify with it," she says. "To *feel* tragedy I must have a story. If not, I prefer a purely abstract idea where I can let fly my imagination." This portrait was taken in 1956, before she had arrived at that personal conclusion.

Above: The Queen of the Swans. With her, the four cygnets who perform the *pas de quatre* that was added to the ballet by Anatole Vilsak for the Diaghilev Ballets Russes. The variation was reinstated in our day by George Balanchine.

Above, right: Odile at work, deceiving the prince. On the film set in Havana, 1968.

"Beauty too rich for use, for earth too dear."

Shakespeare: *Romeo and Juliet*

In the following two pages we see her in her latest Juliet, Alberto Alonso's entirely new ballet, set to music by Berlioz with a score by Pierre Henri. After several previews, it was premiered in its definitive form on March 18, 1970, at Havana's Lorca theatre. In our opinion, this is the most intellectual danced version of the tragedy of the youthful lovers of Verona. The choreographer has cut deeply into the fabric and psychology of society to expose the forces with which it is capable of destroying its own harvest of love, beauty, selflessness and innocence. There is a play within a play in Alonso's *A Tapestry for Romeo and Juliet*, as he entitles his new work. Echoing the drama, a battle of symbols is acted by a group of medieval country minstrels, representing the base passions which engulf and destroy the star-crossed lovers from the start; greed, cowardice, envy, hypocrisy, despotism. . . . The effect is devastating. Never has the assassination of the best there is in Man, as portrayed in ballet, seemed crueler or more gratuitous. By the time Juliet awakes in the crypt and picks up Romeo's dagger, we are being indicted for her tragedy, and humanity's, and . . . our own. Alicia's Lalique-like Juliet is the essence of the Romanesque heroine; gently mysterious in the stances of the era, delightfully ingenuous in her covert raptures, touchingly pathetic in her ultimate desperation. Costumes and décor for the production were designed by Salvador Fernández, and Cuba's fencing champion, Manuel Boada, devised some pretty exciting fireworks for the romping braggarts of both "plagued houses."

Her first Juliet, circa 1944, in Antony Tudor's version staged for the American Ballet Theatre, with costumes and décor by Eugene Berman and the music of Frederick Delius. To this day, at the first evocative five notes which open *Over the Hills and Far Away*, this seldom performed *Romeo and Juliet* comes to mind. It was premiered at the Metropolitan Opera House on April 6, 1943, with Markova as Juliet and Tudor himself playing Tybalt. Later, the starring role

was shared by Alicia Alonso and Nora Kaye, with Hugh Laing as their most dramatic Romeo and occasionally with a youthfully exuberant John Kriza for partner. Whether by design or by coincidence, it seemed that every time that Alicia played Juliet, Fernando, her husband, would play Mercutio, once prompting their daughter Laura—then a little girl— to whisper nervously on our lap, "I hate this one. You'll see, they both die in it!"

Between the years 1948 and 1955, Alicia toured intermittently in Latin America with her own company, first known as Ballet Alicia Alonso and later renamed Ballet de Cuba. It was composed mostly of American and Cuban dancers, and invariably a world-renown *danseur* shared the star billing, in this case Igor Youskevitch, seen here in Havana in 1950, in the last *pas de deux* of Tudor's *Romeo and Juliet*. It is the British choreographer's most sensuous and tender variation for this ballet, corollary to the nuptial scene, the parting kiss of the now wise lovers on the dawn after good Friar Laurence has performed the secret marriage. This is the last time that Romeo and his bride will see each other alive and awake. Greed, envy, hypocrisy and despotism would soon win their Pyrrhic victory in Verona.

"How glorious it is—and also how painful—
to be exceptional."

Alfred de Musset: *Le Merle Blanc.*

La Belle Epoque:
American Ballet Theatre

This historic picture was taken by Irving Penn for *Vogue* in 1947. The royal family of American Ballet Theatre: Perched on the scaffold, from left to right: *danseurs* Hugh Laing, John Kriza, and Igor Youskevitch. More or less on terra firma, left to right: ballerinas Muriel Bentley and Alicia Alonso; British choreographer Antony Tudor; co-director and designer Oliver Smith; dancer-regisseur Dimitri Romanoff; co-director, dancer, and alma mater of the company Lucia Chase; ballerina Nora Kaye, and conductor Max Goberman.

A lovely *Constantia* with Igor Youskevitch, a ballet
in three movements by American dance-choreogra-
pher William Dollar. It was premiered in New York
on October 1944 by Ballet International, with Dollar
himself in the leading male role, and revived in
1946 for the Original Ballet Russe company at the
Metropolitan Opera house, with André Eglevsky

and Rosella Hightower. In 1947 it joined the repertoire of American Ballet Theatre. The work is set to Chopin's Piano Concerto in F Minor, which the composer dedicated in 1836 to his much-admired Constantia Gladowska. Although the ballet is named for her, it does not follow a biographical line. The romantic piece echoes Chopin's brilliant concerto.

In Antony Tudor's *Undertow* Alicia played the role
of Ate, a deceptively innocent-looking dissolute
teenager. She found a magnificent foil in Hugh
Laing's introspective, tortured Transgressor. This
"modern psychological ballet" was premiered at the
Metropolitan on April, 1945. Here, the drunken
women separate the transient lovers against
Raymond Reinin's foreboding backdrop.

Left: Alonso as Mademoiselle Grisi in *Pas de Quatre*. When she became the company's *assoluta*, she was given the leading role in this ballet, that of Mme. Taglioni, whose first interpreter in our day was Alicia Markova, for whom the romantic work was revived.

Below: The historic first performance of Anton Dolin's production of *Pas de Quatre* at New York's Majestic Theatre, February 16th, 1941. Left to right: Alonso, in the role of Carlotta Grisi; Nana Gollner, as Mme. Taglioni, the leading ballerina of the time depicted in this romantic tableau vivant; Irina Baronova visiting backstage with choreographer Dolin; Katherine Sergava as Fanny Cerito; and Nina Stroganova in the role of Lucile Grahn, Danish ballerina.

During the mid-forties, American Ballet Theatre was fortunate to have two formidable choices for the role of Zemphira, the Russian gypsy girl in Massine's *Aleko*: the fiery Nora Kaye, of Russian descent, and a voluptuous and provocative Alicia Alonso, seen here with Russian-born Igor Youskevitch as Aleko, the Stranger. The ballet was inspired by Pushkin's narrative poem, *The Gypsies*, and set to the music of Tchaikowsky's Trio in A Minor. A highlight of the work was Chagall's brilliant décor. Amidst this compendium of Slavic genius, the Cuban ballerina felt quite comfortable. "I just thought of all I had been told and read about Spanish gypsies, first cousins to their Russian counterpart."

An early *Bluebird* variation, with a burnished and
adolescent-looking Youskevitch. She still enameled
her nails red in those days. Later on—as
La Argentinita had concluded long before—she and
other ballerinas realized that, seen from a distance,
the fashionable practice seemed to rob their
fingers of desired length.

Caprichos, by Herbert Ross, was inspired by Goya's series of etchings of the same name. As the curtain falls a voice says in Spanish: "The sleep of reason produces monsters," one of the Great Aragonese's calls to sanity in post-Napoleonic Spain. The version produced by La Argentinita was more effective but it died with her in 1945.

She was twenty when she played
the Mother in *Billy the Kid* with
Eugene Loring, its choreographer,
in the title role. This American
folk tale, based on frontier days,
is set to Aaron Copland's music
on a libretto by Lincoln Kirstein.

In *Theme and Variations* George Balanchine gave ballet one of its greatest abstract classic works. It was premiered at New York's City Center on November 26, 1947, with Alonso and Youskevitch. It has never left their repertoire since; with it they made ballet history throughout the world. The ballet presents a series of magnificent variations for principals and soloists, culminating in the polonaise with the whole company. It is danced to Tchaikowsky's stirring Suite No. 3 in G. Wherever she may be, whatever she is doing, if someone hums the opening bars, Alicia stops and smiles in recognition, as if reminded of her own theme.

The famous "mute cry" after the double crime, in Agnes de Mille's *Fall River Legend*,
based on the Lizzie Borden case. The role of the New England spinster who killed her
father and stepmother with an axe was created for Nora Kaye. But, the 1948 spring
season was in full swing at the Metropolitan, programs had been issued announcing the
premiere, and . . . Nora was ailing in a hospital. In a matter of a few days Alicia was made
ready to substitute for her, creating a furor of controversy in the company. The ballet was
an instant success. Soon it had another round of praise, when Nora was well enough to
take over her role. Thereafter, she shared it with Alicia on occasion, much to the dismay
of Kaye fans. Each gave a totally different interpretation, both magnificent ones. Nora's
was more psychopathic, closer to the insanity of which Lizzie's insensitive stepmother
(very effectively played by Lucia Chase) was accusing her. Alonso's was more pathetic;
that of a lonely, frightened woman who sees her youth and scant chances for happiness
wasted away in the meaningless symbols of a puritanical milieu.

The idea takes tangible shape.   One last confrontation with the stepmother (Lucia Chase).

One of the most versatile *danseurs* on the American Ballet Theatre roster in the forties and fifties was John Kriza, an American of Czechoslovakian ancestry. His young sailor in *Fancy Free* was unforgettable. He was a wild, boisterous, and thoroughly human *Billy the Kid.* He is seen here in that role, with Alicia as the Mexican Sweetheart.

Don Quixote pas de deux, a virtuoso piece which demands great verve and elegance of its interpreters. Alonso and Kriza added a kind of sophisticated bravado that reflected the crisp tempi of Minkus' music.

Left: Two of the puppets in Fokine's *Petrouchka*: Alicia as Ballerina, and Dimitri Romanoff as the Moor. This is the story of a show that plays in Russian fairs. As the puppets dance for the crowd, a drama is lived by them which escapes the puppet-master. Petrouchka is in love with Ballerina, who taunts him with her flirtations with the Moor. In a fit of jealousy, the Moor kills Petrouchka and runs away with Ballerina. The murder creates an uproar of indignation in the crowd. Someone calls for a policeman. Fearing a drop in business—or worse, an arrest—the puppeteer quickly explains that, after all, they are only dolls. But, as he drags the diminishing Petrouchka away in a wake of sawdust, the soul of the murdered puppet rises to curse the puppet master for condemning his captive dolls to lifelessness. Petrouchka was one of Nijinsky's most famous roles. This year (1970) the American Ballet Theatre is presenting a new production of the ballet, retaining the original Stravinsky score.

Above: A rare *Waltz Academy*, with a very young Alonso in eyelet batiste, showing her not fully developed teenager legs.

The handsome American *danseur*,
Royes Fernández, was one of
Alicia's favorite partners in
Coppélia. This is a 1960 photo
taken during Alicia's last
appearance in the United States.

Coppélia in Los Angeles' Greek Theatre, 1957, with André Eglevsky, another great *danseur* who partnered Alonso in her own companies as well as in the American Ballet Theatre. Biels Bjorn Larsen is Dr. Coppelius.

Rehearsing for Carmelita Maracci's *Circo de España*. The Uruguayan choreographer staged this work for Alonso with American Ballet Theatre. It was premiered at the Metropolitan Opera House on April 18, 1951.

Left: As the downcast applicant who has
failed in her audition, in *On Stage!* with
Michael Kidd, creator of this one-act
ballet, playing the Handyman who amuses
and encourages her to dance for him. This
time she dances beautifully, to the
amazement and delight of the "producers"
who are watching from somewhere in the
darkened theatre. Needless to say, the girl
is engaged immediately. Set to music by
Norman dello Joio, this is Kidd's only
ballet; most of his work has been seen in
films and musical comedies.

Right: As the Italian super-*assoluta* in the
humorous *Gala Performance*, a role in
which Muriel Bentley excelled. In this
Tudor creation set to Prokofieff's Classical
Symphony, Nora Kaye as the Russian
ballerina and Janet Reed as the French
soubrette were unforgettable.

Opposite: The *entrechats* in the second
act of *Giselle,* taken during a performance
with American Ballet Theatre. More about
Alonso's *Giselle* in a separate section of
this book.

No one has been able to identify this picture for certain. Alicia believes it was taken in the costume she wore in Tudor's *Lilac Garden*, although she admits that the flowers on her hair seem to be mimosas, rather than the expected spray of lilacs.

Fernando Alonso as Mercutio, in the American Ballet Theatre production of Tudor's *Romeo and Juliet*, 1948. He is now director general of Cuba's National Ballet. Cecil Beaton took this portrait at the Metropolitan Opera House, against one of Eugene Berman's designs for the ballet.

Ingrid e Roberto Rossellini si congratulano colle danzatrici del Balletto Americano la sera dell'inaugurazione del Teatro di Via Manzoni a Milano.

Above: During Ballet Theatre's performances in Germany, Munich's *Heute* had Alicia and Youskevitch on the cover.

Right: The cover of Milan's *La Settimana*, with Ingrid Bergman and Roberto Rossellini greeting the company after a performance. Alicia is seen, far left, in her black swan tutu and tiara. At the extreme right, Nora Kaye, still in Lizzie Borden's cape.

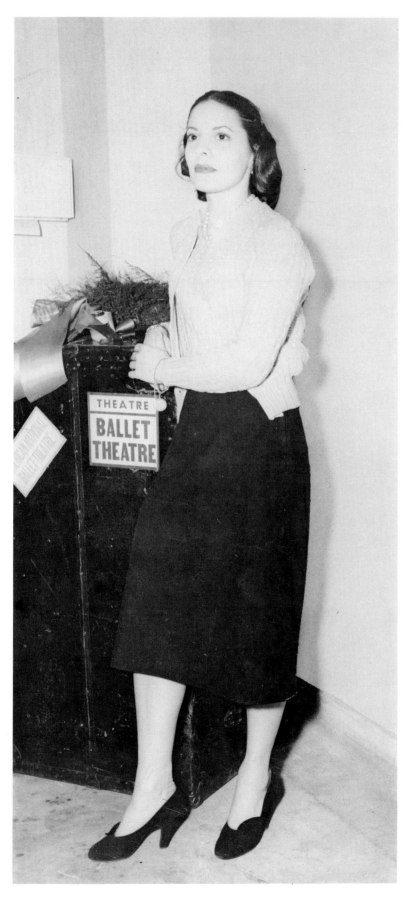

In 1946 she toured Europe for the first time with the American Ballet Theatre. Here she is in the dressing room after the last performance of the New York season, getting her trunk ready.

Alonso in Carmen

The only argument that has been raised is whether Alonso is "the perfect Carmen" or "the perfect Giselle"

— Olga Maynard

Once again the most beguiling female in Spanish lore is the model for what seems destined to be a durable work of art: Alberto Alonso's ballet, *Carmen*. Since the middle of the XIX century the Andalusian seductress—sung about then in the lowly bars and port taverns of Spain under the name of La Petenera—has inspired Merimée's rambling novel, Bizet's opera, one of García Lorca's ballads *(Ballad of the Black Sorrow)*, and Roland Petit's ballet.

Choreographer Alonso first set up his *Carmen* in 1967 for Maya Plisetskaya at the Bolshoi. Judging by the excitement generated by her performances of it in Moscow and London, this entirely new *Carmen* is here to stay.

The formidable task of turning Bizet's opera into a ballet was first achieved successfully by Roland Petit. It was an extremely effective but rather theatrical version, one which offered a magnificent vehicle for Zizi Jeanmaire. Alonso's is a more balletic work. Rather than tell the story in direct narrative form, he has aimed at a deeper intellectual vein. He strikes it by creating an environment and proceeding to reveal the passions which trap and finally destroy the characters.

Alonso places his Carmen in a bull ring, besieged by inexorable symbols of her fate rather than the game. Here the bull is destiny, the bullfighter is life, the spectators the executioner, and José the lover is death. (How Spanish can we get?) The tension is prophetic, even in the tenderly intricate *pas de deux* which precedes the embrace with Don José, or in the stalking panther-grace with which Carmen and the matador weave their erotic play. Evoking a conventicle of the Holy Office of the Inquisition, a semi-circle of masked gypsies witness Carmen's self-immolation, until in a sinister orgy of *zapateado* they seal her fate.

In Alicia Alonso's interpretation (the only one we have seen) this Carmen soars to rarefied heights where the dance becomes poetry in motion. At times, in the sparse russet fringes and jet tassels of her two minicostumes, she seems to turn into the living sculpture of a flame. We are confronted by an Alicia transformed from the sickly, spectral Giselle into a voluptuous flower of flesh that seeks both roots and liberation in love and finds them only in death. Roaming the bull ring, in search of the echo of her lonely soul in every male shadow she can taunt, she is exuberant with the dark essence of the Spanish gypsy—the one that Goya would have captured so magnificently if the Majas of the Court had not possessed him. Gradually we are challenged, bewitched, incensed, and moved to compassion by this obstinate vixen bent on getting her death-wish. Her final token of redemption—a subtle caress to Don José as she falls mortally wounded by him—gives the feeling of being rather than the last flutter of a dove the first wingsweep of some triumphant bird. The curtain falls instantly, but we are exonerated of our own guilt, convinced that Carmen at last has found liberation.

Alberto Alonso has created a fiery ode to the rebellious human spirit—erratic, solitary, vulnerable, but nevertheless grandiose in the end, transfigured by love and sorrow and belated awareness of all that life has meant. Seeing his *Carmen* unfold step by step—in spite of the all-pervading Bizet score—we realized how much more his psychological portrait owes to Lorca then to Merimée. In his *Ballad of the Black Sorrow* the Spanish poet gave Carmen the more typically Andalusian name of Soledad Montoya, the gypsy of "thighs of anemones and breasts like smoky anvils moaning round songs," the mysterious vagrant who comes down from the hills at dawn smelling of manly shadows, searching for "her person and her joy," only to run like a wild stallion that "finally meets the sea and is swallowed by the waves."

We even think that, consciously or not, Alonso went with and to Lorca beyond the character of Carmen-Soledad in his ballet. In the performance that we saw Alicia was magnificently partnered by Azari Plisetski who as Don José imparted a new depth to this otherwise one-dimensional role. Here again the choreography evokes Lorca. We could almost hear the words as José at last wraps a prone Carmen tenderly in his arms: "Bathe your body in water of the larks and leave your heart in peace, Soledad Montoya."

The role of Escamillo, the bullfighter, was played this time by Cuban *danseur* Roberto Rodríguez. He was resplendent in white silk and a kind of fatalistic, Grecian self-assurance. (After all, the game began in Crete.) Seeing his controlled, elegant power—so remote from the Iberian cockiness flaunted usually in this role—we were reminded of another Lorca poem, the one he wrote at the death of his beloved friend, the matador Ignacio Sánchez Mejías: "Like a river of lions his marvelous strength, as a torso of marble his wisdom was etched." But then, we're Spanish, not French. So was *Carmen*.

The Cuban production of Alonso's *Carmen* was the highlight of Mexico's Cultural Olympics which preceded the international games of 1968. We saw it earlier that year in Havana, at a gala performance for the 600 delegates of Cuba's Cultural Congress whose British Delegation was headed by Arnold Haskell and Sir Herbert Read.

T. de G.

Stills from the film version of Alberto Alonso's ballet *Carmen* produced in color and CinemaScope by the Cuban Film Institute (ICAIC), Havana 1968. Music by Bizet, reorchestrated by Rodion Schedrin. Decor by Boris Messener, costumes by Salvador Fernández.

Cast: Carmen, Alicia Alonso; José, Azari Plisetski; matador Escamillo, Roberto Rodríguez; Col. Zúñiga, Hugo Guffanti; Destiny, Josefina Méndez. Locale: Seville 1846, bull ring and gypsy ghetto.

"The beaks of cockerels dig
   seeking the aurora·
   when she descends from the dark hills.
   Whom do you want,
   alone, and at this hour?
   What business is it of yours?
   I look for what I am looking,
   for my person and my joy."

"Gleaming copper, her flesh
  smells of steed and shadow.
Smoky anvils, her breasts
  are moaning round songs."

"While the river sings below
and the new light weaves a wreath
with blossoms of the calabash."

"Bathe your body in water of the larks
and let your heart be in peace."

"The living sculpture of a flame."

"Adieu, Joselito."   *"Bon jour, Matador."*

"Stallion that runs away
  finally meets with the sea
  and is swallowed by the waves."

"You are turning black as jet
 in flesh and soul.
 Where are your linen chemises!
 O, your thighs of anemones!"

"O, sorrow of the gypsy people,
sorrow clean and always lone.
O, sorrow of hidden stream
and far, faraway dawn."

Taking her bows at the Bolshoi with Plisetski, 1969. "Theseus' partner in the Cretan ring."

Open letter to Alicia Alonso

Dearest Alicia, Odette-Odile-Carmen-Giselle,

You are Everywoman, the bewitching and the bewitched, peasant and princess, gentle and caressing, cruel with a look that carries darts. As a white cloud you float across the stage, you rise from your partner's arms, weightless.

Yet you have muscles of steel, you can dazzle us with tricks that are no longer tricks when you do them. You make the complex seem simple, time like gravity defies its laws for you, detail becomes fused into a magnificent whole. You make music visible, your bow is an ode.

With you, all critic's phrases are meaningless. How can you interpret Giselle when you are Giselle?

Your work will continue long after you have ceased to dance. Generations of dancers will have been enriched through watching you, just as you yourself have drawn from the tradition handed down by Taglioni and Pavlova.

Cuba is fortunate to possess you; you belong to the world, and are already an immortal in the history of our great art.

Alicia, I salute you, with warm affection as a friend and with profound admiration as a critic.

Arnold Haskell

"She was born so
Giselle would not die."
Fernando Emery, Buenos Aires, 1959

In November of 1969, Alonso celebrated one of the most important anniversaries of her career: twenty-five years of dancing *Giselle*. Viktor Rona, Bulgaria's *premier danseur*, was brought to Cuba for the occasion to partner her in three commemorative performances at Havana's García Lorca theatre. They are seen here, in the dress rehearsal for Act I.

Opposite below: The Cuban star, receiving an ovation at the end of the opening gala performance.

Rehearsing with Danish *premier danseur* Flemming Flindt in Copenhagen, October 1969, when she was invited by the Royal Danish Ballet to dance *Giselle*. Of that performance, Denmark's *Berlingske Tidende* said: "Alonso in *Giselle* will remain forever as one of the greatest experiences in ballet today."

In the second act the spirit of the deceived peasant girl emerges from her grave to save her beloved Prince Albrecht from the terrible punishment that the Wilis reserve for faithless lovers: to dance to death.

Alonso's 1969 formal portrait as Giselle in Act II. The romantic ballet, written in 1840 by Théophile Gautier, was inspired by a German legend first recorded by the poet Heinrich Heine. It offers one of the most challenging roles in classical ballet. Giselle must be both a formidable technician and a sensitive actress. Of necessity, the first requisite calls for a mature dancer. And yet, to play the girl in love convincingly, she must project innocence and youth. Then, as the dead maiden come to life temporarily in Act II, she must possess a kind of crystalline beauty while expressing deep feelings of love and grief for her repentant, faithless lover. To this day, Alonso remains one of the ideal interpreters of this demanding role.

The carefree peasant girl and Prince Albrecht in their courting games of the first act. Two stills from the full-length film of the ballet, produced in 1964 by the Cuban Film Institute, with Azari Plisetski partnering Alicia. An elegant young *danseur noble,* Plisetski is the brother of Russia's *assoluta,* Maya Plisetskaya. He first went to Cuba as a guest of the National Ballet. He soon fell in love with the tropical island and, eventually, with the company's lyrical ballerina, Loipa Araujo. Maya came from Moscow for the wedding in Havana, at which Alicia and Fernando Alonso gave the bride away, with the entire company in attendance.

Her first, historic *Giselle*, with British
danseur and choreographer Anton
Dolin, in the American Ballet Theatre
production, 1943. After a year off stage
following three eye operations, upon
her return to work Alicia was asked to
substitute for the company's then
ailing guest star, British *assoluta*
Markova. It was a tremendous challenge
for the Cuban ballerina. Within a few
days' rehearsal she was ready to take
over the role she had been dreaming
of while convalescing. "At once I
forgot those long hours in a dark
room listening to a recording of Adam's
music. Suddenly the music was there,
full and alive, for me to dance to.
And there was Anton's firm, strong hand
pulling me away from Giselle's
hut. . . . You forget who you are when
you become Giselle. There are
moments, in the second act, when
you even forget who *she* was! You
become all of young humanity forgiving
itself for being, well . . . human."

In 1948 Eugene Berman was commissioned to design new costumes and décor for the American Ballet Theatre's *Giselle*. It turned out to be a rather unconventional departure, with the Wilis, the dead maidens, in blue tutus and black trimmings. Alicia is seen here against Berman's surrealistic backdrop for Act I. Since then, the company has reverted to traditional white tutus and Corot-inspired décor.

Youskevitch and Alonso, the incomparable interpreters of Albrecht and Giselle. There was something luminous and at the same time deeply convincing about their performance of this work, pervadingly romantic as it is. One *believed* the injudicious prince in his irrepressible fascination for the mountain maiden. One *believed* in her total surrender to her first and only love; above all, in her faith in him—posing, as we know he is, as a common stranger who takes her away from her humble home duties and her peace with the false promise of everlasting love. And then, in the moment of reckoning and truth, one *believed* in her eternal forgiveness, and in his profound, belated knowledge of all that this now lost love has meant for him. Who can forget Alonso's adieu upon re-entering the grave, or the tragic, prostrate figure at her feet, Youskevitch—his temples slighly greyed for the second act—shrouding his grief in an immense black cloak?

Alonso is the first ballerina of the
Western world to have been invited
by the Soviet Union to dance *Giselle*,
which until then, in the Russia of our
century, was a kind of exclusive
privilege of Russian ballerinas. It
happened in 1957, some years before
the Cuban Revolution and the
subsequent alliances between Cuba and
the Socialist nations, at the time when
Alicia was firmly established as the
United States' *assoluta*. In Leningrad
she was partnered by Vladilen
Semyonov, the Kirov Ballet's *premier
danseur*. We see them here at
rehearsal, in the first *pas de deux* of
the ballet, and sharing their bows
with the conductor, at the end.

During a second visit to the Soviet
Union, 1958, Moscow's *Theatre Week*
magazine ran a cover story on her
famous *Giselle*.

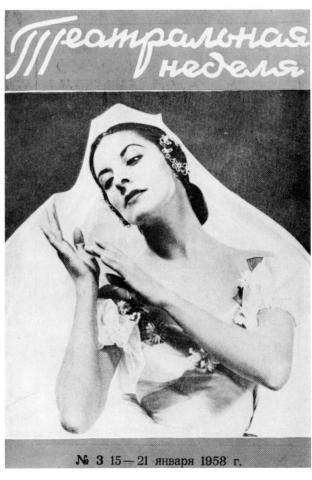

Театральная
неделя

№ 3 15—21 января 1958 г.

Giselle's mad scene
at various stages
of Alonso's career.

Havana, November 1969, in a
gala performance of the ballet,
partnered by Bulgarian *premier
danseur* Viktor Rona.

At Los Angeles' Greek Theatre,
1957.

With the Bolshoi, Moscow 1958.

New Orleans-born Royes Fernández
was one of her most handsome partners
in *Giselle*. On two separate long
seasons, (1948-50 and 1952-54) they
toured Central and South America with
her own company, to the delight of
audiences who took pride in their
kinship to these two Latin exponents
of a basically European art. Alicia and
Royes had a very happy association
on and off stage. There was always
much laughter and Spanish chatter
going on between them. It was with
Royes as Prince Siegfried that Alicia,
with her own ballet company, launched
a new staging of *Swan Lake* by British
choreographer Mary Skeaping, in
Havana, 1953.

During her first tour of the Soviet
Union, 1957, Latvian *danseur* Harald
Rittenberg danced *Giselle* with her in
the city of Riga.

"Her bow is an ode"
— Arnold Haskell, 1967.

Alonso stands unique among her peers for her creative and protean bows. In her, they are not merely improvised corollaries to the performance. The performance is over. A little of us has died with Juliet or Giselle; the Swan Queen is happily embracing her prince with the arms of a real girl; by the stroke of a knife Carmen has been banished forever from Seville. Now Alicia belongs to us. Unhampered by the costume—indeed, enhanced by it, since all of them seem so inherently hers— she proceeds to communicate her personal moods directly to us. First there may be a simple lowering of the head, arms limp at her sides, no nonsense with the feet; this is the thinker in profound reverence of a miracle that cannot be defined. She snaps out of her introspective awe to grasp her partner's hands and share the gift. Next time around she will stop suddenly in flight and look up high, searching the galleries. For a moment she seems lost, but just as quickly, she falls smiling to her knee—not like a ballerina, but like a lonely girl who has found a friend in a huge crowd. She will stoop as low as she can gracefully to carry on a silent exchange of nods and signs with the fans straining at orchestra's edge, the cryptic dialogue between the young and the great. (What on earth are they telling each other?) There may be an ultimate salute in which she runs out swiftly straight at us. When we think she's going to fly right off the stage, she stops and stands erect, stretching on half-toe, back arched, wide open arms seeming to send her heart off to us. And then, that small figure vibrating with beauty and life force, becomes Theseus' partner in the Cretan ring, not as much our captive as her art's. We have asked her about her bows. Does she plan them? Are they part of a pattern, a design? Subconsciously, perhaps. She does give them some thought. But finally, when time comes to execute them, you, history, the moment, the punishment and joys that have led to the encounter, are the unsung choreographers of these token encores. On this page she is seen at the Bolshoi; above, with Vladilen Semyonov.

T. de G.

The Critics

One of the greatest dancers of this generation.
—Olivier Merlin, *Le Monde*, Paris 1966

The summit of a perfection we believed impossible.
—Sebastian Gasch, *Destino*, Barcelona 1969

It takes no great seer to prophesy that she will occupy her place in line with Pavlova and Markova as a great classic dancer.
—John Martin, *The New York Times*, 1941

A superlatively beautiful Giselle.
—*The Globe and Mail*, Toronto 1967

She is magnificent. We could perceive her mysterious and perfect etheriality.
—Peter Williams, *Ballet Today*, London 1965

Her dancing is something marvelously classic and organic. I bow to her art.
—Galina Ulanova, *News from Moscow*, 1969

Alonso will remain forever as one of the rarest experiences in ballet.
—*Berlingske Tidende*, Copenhagen 1969

Technically perfect, dramatically forceful and very much human. One of the greatest ballerinas in the world.
—*Daily Express*, London 1953

Her Giselle has the chiaroscuro of finely veined marble.
—Don McDonagh, *The New York Times*, 1967

That miracle of vision dances, and as she does we know what it is to dance, and to dance perfectly. The prima ballerina of the world.

—*El Dia,* Mexico 1968

A brilliant and deeply moving performance by Alonso in *Giselle* brought a rousing ovation from last night's audience at the Metropolitan.

—Louis Biancolli,
The New York World-Telegram, 1960

She does not make one movement void of psychological content. This brings poetry to the movement. One of the greatest performers of our time.

—Arnold Haskell, *El Mundo,* Havana 1967

Many of us consider her the greatest contemporary dancer.

—Ann Barzel, *Chicago American,* 1955

She stops our breath with her virtuosity.

—*La Libre Belgique,* Brussels 1969

Supreme command of the stage, musicality, purity of style.

—Sylvia de Nussac, *L'Express,* Paris 1969

Alicia Alonso danced Giselle with such intensity as perhaps has never been equaled in this famous role.

—*Variety,* New York 1967

Since Pavlova no other ballerina has aroused such enthusiasm in Berlin audiences.

—*Tageblatt,* Berlin 1953

She perceives the vibration of music in space; she herself lives the dramatic substance of music.

—*Soviet Culture,* 1967

Once we called Alonso a feather. Now we call her a feather with the strength of steel. Beautiful, prodigious.

—*Il Gazzetino,* Venice 1953

The lyricism of her voluptuous *Carmen* escapes the laws of the dance to a radiant mastery.

—Henri Berthold, *Relax,* Brussels 1969

Artistic grandeur shines on her. At once, spectacular and pure.

—*Leipziger Volzeitung,* Leipsig 1969

The greatest ballerina in contemporary ballet.

—A. Daschieva, *Soviet Culture,* 1969

One of the finest ballerinas in the world.

—Ebbe Mork, *Politiken,* Copenhagen 1969

Brilliance and artistry in her performance of Giselle.

—Miles Kastendieck
New York Journal-American, 1960

The greatest ballerina in the world.

—*Il Mattino di Napoli,* 1953

Not only an extraordinary dancer but an admirable actress.

—*La Dernière Heure,* Brussels 1969

Her Giselle will be historical.

—Rene Sirvin, *L'Aurore,* Paris 1965

Alicia at home

Alicia pays a morning visit to a class
for junior ballerinas. The ballet
mistress in this case, far left, is Mirta
Pla, herself one of Cuba's prima
ballerinas. She was outstanding as the
Queen of the Wilis in the Cuban film
production of *Giselle*.

After attending Cuba's homage to its National Ballet in 1967, Premier Castro listens attentively while Alicia talks backstage. Just behind her, next to Azari Plisetski, we get a glimpse of Mirta García's swarthy beauty. This petite ballerina won second prize and silver medal at Varna's 1966 International Dance Festival.

When an American correspondent arrives at the studio, everyone stops to chat, mostly to ask questions about ballet in the United States. Cuba receives all sorts of magazines from all over the world, but American publications seldom reach there by mail.

Above: Jorge Esquivel, Cuba's budding *danseur noble*, in the title role of Balanchine's *Apollo,* partnering Laura Alonso, Terpsichore, muse of the dance. He is seen at left with muses Thalia and Calliope, played by Marta García and the Mexican-born Clara Carranco.

At Varna's International Dance Festival of 1968, the then eighteen-year-old Esquivel elicited such raves from European critics as "the world's youngest promise of another Youskevitch." At the age of nine he had been selected for a ballet career among the wards of the now non-existent Havana orphanage. "I didn't know what ballet was," he says today in his soft, diffident tones. "I thought it was something athletic and challenging and I just hoped that the doctors and teachers who came to examine us would take me." Eventually he became one of the star pupils of the national ballet school and as such was drafted for the ballet company. By now he partners Alicia with the brilliance and aplomb of polished steel, although he is disarmingly unassuming of his precocious gifts: form, power *cum* lightness, and a handsome stage presence. He still attends prep school, one step ahead of his non-dancing teenaged fiancée.

Above: Stars and soloists in a morning run. Leaping, left to right, is Loipa Araujo (now Mrs. Azari Plisetski) and just behind her, Uranis Urbino. In the center, Mirta Pla and Alicia. Last one on the right is Menia Martínez, now on loan to Maurice Béjart's ballet in Brussels. Resting at the barre are Clara Carranco—a Mexican who has been with the Cuban ballet since 1960—and soloist Marta García.

Opposite: The nine to twelve year-old class at Havana's ballet school, conducted by ballerina Mirta Pla, right of the column. In the summer they wear white batiste rehearsal togs. In winter, everyone dons regulation black leotards.

A group of twelve to fourteen-year-old scholarship students. If they make it this far, they are allowed to perform with the ballet company in "crowd" scenes. They come from all walks of life, after a rigorous selection among hundreds of applicants. They live and study at an art school city called Cubanacán—the former residential section, the Country Club. Scholarship students are housed in the palatial homes of Cuba's departed rich, alongside with those who stayed. A matron, called "Granny" regardless of her age, tends to them and acts as house mother and chaperone. Ballet training is taken concurrently with regular school subjects, with beginning French and music added to the curriculum.

The top echelon of Cuban ballerinas, in
a class conducted by the company's
director general, Fernando Alonso. Left
to right: Aurora Bosch behind Mirta Pla;
the temporarily absent Menia Martínez,
loaned to Maurice Béjart for his Twentieth
Century Ballet in Brussels; behind Alicia's
arm is Loipa Araujo, and next to her,
Josefina Méndez, one of the finest dancers
that Cuban ballet has produced.

Bach's Mass in B Minor is the music for Cuba's latest ballet production: *Bach plus Eleven*, with choreography by José Parés. Outstanding in this work are the Kyrie and the Gloria, performed by *premier danseur* Alberto Méndez and soloist Marta García. The work, premiered in Havana in April 1970, at first caused a small flurry of controversy. On one side were those who thought that Bach and the Mass were being profaned by the association with this daring and earthy ballet. On the other, some—not necessarily non-believers—considered this work as a tribute to the composer, and a desirable human approach to the Mass. The majority of Cuban intellectuals think it is a healthy sign of a successful revolution to have both a departure in classical ballet forms —rare in most Socialist countries—and a frank encounter with religious themes and music.

"Should we call this picture, 'Trilby and Svengali'?" we asked Alicia. "No!" she burst out, in what we thought was going to be a protest. "Call it 'Simon Legree and a slave.' That'd be more like it!" she finished, laughing. Actually, Fernando comes in to observe for fine points and make suggestions only in the final stages of her rehearsals.

Unaware that he was providing a historic picture, one morning Fernando Alonso got to class too late to change his *miliciano* uniform. He had been on guard duty all night. No one seemed to mind the regulation pistol still at his belt; a ballet class was waiting for him, and that's all that counted. Every civilian in Cuba, from fifteen to sixty, women included, serves with a branch of the armed forces and handles firearms. Duties are assigned loosely, to permit everyone to carry on regular activities.

Alicia at home, December 1969.

173

174

The long-legged colt looking down is *danseur* Jorge Esquivel in 1964. Two places behind him are Raul Bustabad and Edmundo Ronquillo, black students who became soloists with Cuba's National Ballet.

New girls trying their balance after the first lessons. At this point, prior to formal acceptance into the school, they are closely observed in order to weed out the mere hopeful from the talented. Ballet has become one of the most desirable careers for both girls and boys in revolutionary Cuba. Gone are the old prejudices about boys "dancing" and girls "going on the stage."

Full scholarship ballet students showing Alicia new additions to their little museum of natural history at the School City. Besides ballet classes and regular school duties, boys get daily military training. It is curious to see them marching up and down a shady avenue, in boots and olive green uniform, then rushing into the shower house to come out, all poise and lanky grace, in black tights and practice slippers. Girls curtsey as they pass you in the streets of Cubanacán; boys bow slightly. None of it precludes resumption of their games and scraps the moment your back is turned to them.

Right, above: The handsome and talented Argentinian dancer, Rodolfo Rodríguez, when he was still married to Laura Alonso, chatting with her and an American correspondent in the patio of Havana's ballet studios. For several years Rodolfo was Cuba's *premier danseur*. After his divorce he returned to South America.

Below: Waiting for lunch to be served. From right to left: Rodolfo Rodríguez, Azari Plisetski, a visiting friend, company *regisseur* Sergio Mauri, and Laurita with her back to the camera. In pre-revolutionary days Mauri was a used car salesman. Last time we saw him, December 1969, he was busy cutting sugar cane like a pro. "Some of us must make up for the kids," he said through a newly-grown beard, meaning the dancers. "They're not even allowed to handle a machete; it would develop the wrong muscles. They do other things, like picking fruit and coffee. But this year it's sugar cane that counts most."

This page: A pensive Alicia, also waiting for lunch in the patio, after a long morning's rehearsal.

Alicia in the Cuban production of
Coppélia, with Hugo Guffanti as the
straying Franz. Like Arnold Haskell,
we were a bit apprehensive when we
learned that Alicia was going to dance
the soubrette role of Swanilda, a frivolous
girl who makes fun of an old doll-maker.
From her first entrance we realized we
were going to see a great Alonso
performance. She imparts new depth to
this role, adding special wickedness
to her humorous plot to fool poor old
Dr. Coppelius and win back her lover
Franz. In this ballet, her daughter Laura
leads the spirited czardas.

Far left: The dining room in the building of Havana's ballet studios and offices. Azari Plisetski and Alicia in the foreground, lunching with a visiting friend. In the back, the chef, now a ballet sophisticate who pampers Alicia and the finicky and refuses to serve second helpings to the plump, dancer or not. He manages to produce one of the best noon meals that one can get in Havana for a peso (one dollar). All offices, schools and workshops in Cuba provide a full noontime meal for workers and students. This augments the ration card at home. Children, the sick, and the aged get special cards providing more meat and milk. There are no restrictions on fish and most native vegetables, plentiful in this lush, tropical island. Beef is carefully controlled to permit large export shipments. Cuba sells beef to Spain and Italy. Also, on occasion, Cuban beef is sold at London's Smithfield market.

Left: Fernando Alonso, giving last minute instructions at a dress rehearsal.

Above: Enrique González Mantici, the conductor of Havana's symphony orchestra and musical director of the National Ballet. The company's regular conductor is Manuel Duchesne.

A versatile Alonso, seen here rehearsing *Swan Lake* and performing *La Fille Mal Gardée*, a favorite role of Anna Pavlova. In the Cuban production, José Parés is the designing Maman Simone, a role which is traditionally played by a man.

Cuba's National Art Schools of Cubanacán—the
island's aboriginal name—were the prize exhibit at
the VIII International Congress of Architecture, which
in 1964 convened in Havana. The huge complex of
domed buildings housing schools, workshops and
ancillary installations is a triumphant child of the
American blockade and one of the Revolution's
outstanding achievements. For lack of reinforcing
steel, architects Vittorio Garatti and Ricardo Porro
resorted to the vaulted ceilings built by Catalan
monks in the seventeenth century. To save on
electric power they devised a system of natural air
conditioning—and a safeguard against hurricanes—
which owes much to seraglio lattices and the
Andalusian shutters of colonial days. *Above.* The
approach to the Modern Dance building. *Below:* A
class in progress at the Ballet building. *To the right:*
Fernando Alonso and a foreign correspondent under
one of the new domes belonging to the Music School,
then under construction. All buildings were completed
in 1965 and are now fully active with 7,000 students
from ages nine to seventeen attending classes and
living in the area, formerly Havana's restricted
residential preserve, the Country Club.

Cubanacán's classrooms, work-shops, theatres, music halls, libraries, exhibition galleries and technical installations are surrounded by parks, patios, and terraces, made cool and inviting by center fountains of abstract design. The aim was to create a mood conducive to both, meditation and creation. Classrooms are designed after the Athenian hemicircle, where the teacher stands at the lowest level, and the class sits above. A labyrinth of circular brick walls offering privacy without doors forms the therapy rooms in the dance and theatre compounds. The artists' print shop is a marvel of built-in functionalism. Corridors have strategically placed pedestals and wall niches to display art work. Drinking fountains spout out of miniature jungles growing vertically in wall panels. The noted British architecture critic Diana Roundtree said of Cubanacán in London's *Observer*: "It is a sign that marks the serenity of the Cuban regime that as it fights an economic battle for survival and while the Revolution remains alert, government controlled materials are provided for such unconventional projects as these art schools. It is obvious that the capacity to remain at once serene and vigilant has been invented by the Cubans." In these pages, the porticos and patio of the Painting and Sculpture building, with Ricardo Porro's sculptured fountain at far left.

187

Center: Alicia's latest portraits in
practice attire, December 1969.
The monastic mood contrasts with the
scenes framing these two pages: The
sensuous Miller's wife in *The Three
Cornered Hat*, a very Spanish version of
this ballet produced for Cuba by
Argentinian *danseur* Rodolfo Rodríguez.

"Everything passes. Powerful art alone is eternal. The marble outlasts the citadel."

Theophile Gautier: *L'Art*